Merle Lamprecht

A Christian in London & Paris
Poems

© 2009 by Merle Lamprecht. All rights reserved.

WinePress Publishing (PO Box 428, Enumclaw, WA 98022) functions only as book publisher. As such, the ultimate design, content, editorial accuracy, and views expressed or implied in this work are those of the author.

No part of this publication may be reproduced, stored in a retrieval system, or transmitted in any way by any means—electronic, mechanical, photocopy, recording, or otherwise—without the prior permission of the copyright holder, except as provided by USA copyright law.

No part of this book may be reproduced in any form without permission in writing from the publisher, except in the case of brief quotations embodied in critical articles or reviews.

Scripture references marked NIV on page 127 are taken from the *Holy Bible: New International Version*®. *NIV*®. Copyright © 1973, 1978, 1984 by International Bible Society. Used by permission of Zondervan. All rights reserved.

Scripture references marked KJV on page 127 are taken from the *King James Version* of the Bible.

Scripture references marked NKJV on page 127 are taken from the *New King James Version,* © 1979, 1980, 1982 by Thomas Nelson, Inc., Publishers. Used by permission.

ISBN 13: 978-1-57921-939-0
ISBN 10: 1-57921-939-X
Library of Congress Catalog Card Number: 2007940287

To John,

remembering with love
the many miles we have
walked together over
fifty years

What good will it be
for a man if he gains
the whole world,
yet forfeits his soul?

—Matt 16:26

Contents

LONDON

I was up early 8
What I like about London 10
Chimney pots. 13
A statue in Trafalgar Square 15
We met quite by chance 17
This one wasn't a statue 19
London wouldn't be London 21
Hamley's 24
A traditional tea 27
It really wasn't his day. 30
Christ before the High Priest. 33
London—a gourmet's delight. 36
No Haussmann 39
Piccadilly Circus. 43
The Women of World War II. 45
Berwick Street Market 47
London was suffering. 50
London's basements 52
Diana. 55
Christian art. 58
London's heart 61
When we're back 63
Regent's Park 65
Mid May to mid June. 67

Paris

St-Germain-des-Prés	72
Rushing somewhere	75
Place Dauphine	77
Joan of Arc	79
Roissy-Charles de Gaulle Terminal 2	81
Place des Vosges	83
Clocks	85
Jardin des Plantes	87
Les Égouts	90
Bus 75	91
Early morning walk	93
Hotel	96
A day in Paris	98
Portrait	101
Just consider	103
Citizens	106
Jardin du Luxembourg	108
The Kiss	110
Plaques	112
The new Paris	114
Doors	117
Traffic jam	119
Views	121
Parc de Bagatelle	124
References	127

London

I was up early

I was up
early
we were going
to London
come out here
he said
I'm on the
balcony

it was sunrise
the pink sky
had turned
the sea
dusky pink
the seven palms
stood still
cool
before the
morning's heat
seagulls called
as they
wheeled and whirled
their glad shouts
the only sounds
heard above
the waves
gently breaking
on rocks

A Christian in London & Paris

look at this!
he said
sweeping out
his arm
why do you
want to go
to London?

because
it's not here
I said
because
it's different
because
in London
twirling like
a kaleidoscope
bright
vibrant
shattering
my mind
shall rest

for
God said
six days
you shall labor
and on the
seventh
rest

What I like about London

what I like
about London
he said
are the trees
the birds
the ducks
and the flowers
I added

I can't think
of London
without thinking
of trees
the London Planes
lofty light
softening
grey buildings
arching above
grey streets
the trees
in the parks
majestic
unforgettable
interspersed
with small
relations
white and pink
blossomed
in spring

A Christian in London & Paris

the ancient
leafy tree
propped up
in
Whitehall Gardens
its tired
twisted limbs
statuesque
on the lawn

of birds
singing summer
in the center
of London
and ducklings
ducking in lakes
begging bread
and swans
serenely sailing
the Serpentine

of flowers
swinging in baskets
up Regent Street
pink and yellow
this year
and spilling
from boxes
on window sills
and roses and roses
in Regent's Park
and unpotted flowers
along Flower Walk
and unplanted

A Christian in London & Paris

cow-parsley
ethereally white
swaying beside
the canal

with thousands
of red buses
whirling
like clockwork
with taxis and crowds
clatter and clang

they soften
the city
like
still, still waters
and there
you restore
my soul

Chimney pots

I remember
when I
first flew
into London
half a century
ago
and saw
row upon row
of red-roofed
buildings
stretching
as far as
I could see
and every building
topped
by several
chimney pots

how many
are there
in London?
has anyone
ever counted?
I stare
from my window
into quiet
Craven Street
on to
round rimmed
columns

A Christian in London & Paris

of terracotta clay—
chimney pots
all much the same
the odd tall one
with pigeons
perched on top
one stack
has ten in a row—
there must be
two hundred
in this little street
and the
red-brick buildings
still bear the grime
of the soot
that belched
from them
decades ago
centrally heated
windows replaced
I hope
they never
remove these pots
from
London's face

they remind me
of old Christians
molded from clay
who have served
long and hard
and now
await
their
Lord's Day

A statue in Trafalgar Square

it's fitting
that London's
most meaningful
statue—
not mentioned
in tourist books—
should be there
in the heart
of the city
in Trafalgar Square

it's not Nelson
perched proud
on his column
or Charles the First
on his horse
or the tragic
new marble
symbol of courage

it's the
birth of a baby
in the porch
of a church
it's
Jesus the Christ
Son of God
Word and Lord

A Christian in London & Paris

the concrete plinth
powerful
square
Scripture entwined
pictures that Word
emerging as flesh
from its
turbulent top—
the birth
of our Lord
who lived
with us here
who gave himself
for the crowds
swarming the square

I stood
for a moment
in wonder
there

We met quite by chance

we met
quite by chance
among the statues
in Embankment Gardens
one I knew
slightly
the other
a stranger—
Robert Raikes
and William Tyndale

Robert
was standing
with kindly smile
curling ribboned wig
stepping forward
boldly
Book in hand
behind
in mind's eye
I saw
children stretching
to eternity
children from
all nations
singing
Jesus Christ
is Word
and Lord

A Christian in London & Paris

William
cloaked and capped
was standing where
Henry's palace stood
strangled in mercy
before fire consumed
martyred
in foreign land
for translating the
New Testament
so all
could read

martyred –

for picking up
his pen

This one wasn't a statue

this one
wasn't a statue
standing still
holding a pole
on a
patch of pavement

theater tickets!
McDonald's!
Burger King!
excursions!
diversions!
cheap! free!

does anyone
read what's written
as they
push past?

what a job
I prefer
my frenetic way

and what do
pole-holders
think
standing all day
in the midst
of the crowd?

A Christian in London & Paris

perhaps
they think
of what they saw
on telly last night
of what they'll drink
in the pub tonight

perhaps
like Brother Lawrence
cutting carrots
in priestly kitchen
they
speak to God
as they
stand and stare
on the streets
of London
advertising
lunchtime fare

how dare
I judge them
standing
here?

London wouldn't be London

London
wouldn't be
London
without the Queen

the Queen
was here
yesterday
said a
policewoman
on duty
in The Mall
when I
asked her
what was happening
she was
young and pretty
her filled eyes
showed
how she felt

that esteem
has been
earned
and at
eighty
still is

A Christian in London & Paris

we were
on our way
to the
Queen's Gallery
to see her
new portrait

there she sat
almost filling
the canvas
dressed in green—
a wonderful
vivid emerald—
the pearls
the brooch
somewhat shy
serene

a film
showed the artist
touching
his palette
looking up
adding
layer upon layer
until
the portrait
was finished
realistic
simple
true

A Christian in London & Paris

and I realized
the awesome responsibility
that rests on monarchy—
to do
what is right
in the sight
of the
Lord—

and on us too

Hamley's

Hamley's
was an
old-fashioned
what I would call
a very English shop
when
I first went there
but now
with sleek escalators
gliding swiftly
to the top
it could
sit comfortably
in a
modern mall

but there's
still the thrill
of seeing
tables and tables of toys
look at those dogs
turning somersaults!
here's a handbag
with a girl
on a horse!
look at those cogs
turning round and round!
can't we squash

them in our
hand luggage?
grandparents fill
floppy red bags
let's spoil them
while we may
how
will they cope
in their world
spinning faster
every day?

at the apex
of Regent Street
I see some children—
somewhat older—
on the steps of
All Souls
Langham Place
clutching Bibles
talking, laughing
life on every face
waiting under
Gothic spire
for the Sunday service
to hear your Word
to sing your praise
to learn to do
your will—
these are the children
who have chosen
these are the children
who have hope

A Christian in London & Paris

and I pray
for the children
for whom I shopped—

only by
your grace
will they cope

A traditional tea

a traditional
tea in London
meant for me
in the fifties
Lyon's Corner House
waitresses
in black dresses
frilly white aprons
bustling about
or plate-sized pancakes
rolled
sprinkled with sugar
in a
Pimlico tearoom
or—so sophisticated!
the West End
a cappuccino
with brown sugar
in a thick
ceramic cup

in the nineties
afternoon tea
in the
Ritz Palm Court
pink domed and gold
poised on
delicate chairs
or Brown's—

A Christian in London & Paris

a London country house—
dark paneled
with capacious chairs
the pianist
at the Ritz
played carols
it was
Christmas time
at Brown's
classics decorously
while we ate
cucumber sandwiches
scones and jam
and tiny tiny cakes
some chocolate
touched with gold

but now
in two thousand and six
I prefer the
Orangery
sitting relaxed
on the terrace
under white sunshades
looking at the lawn
the avenue of
cone-shaped trees
eating
wild berry tart
and cream where
Queen Anne
once did
the same

A Christian in London & Paris

but what
of the millions
who don't have dinner?

if I were
a billionaire . . .

I'd better ask
old Mrs. Cummings
to tea

It really wasn't his day

it really
wasn't his day
he'd set off
down The Mall
trailing
his case

small
scruffy
nondescript
he trudged past
spectators
soldiers
security
workers
police
all waiting
expectantly
for the procession
to begin

he'd gone
halfway
was feeling
chuffed
what a chance
he'd taken!

A Christian in London & Paris

we saw him
between
two policemen
soon joined
unobtrusively
by others
in patrol cars

was there a
bomb in his
baggage?—
we'd been
watching workmen
checking drains

but his
case contained
an old blanket
unrolled
it revealed
several small
parcels
at which
he stared
sheepishly

I didn't think
he'd be home
in time for tea
or celebration
with the wife

A Christian in London & Paris

Judas
was a thief
the odd coin
or two—
nothing much—
but drops of
water wear
rocks into
chasms—

drown men too

Christ before the High Priest

Christ before the High Priest
Honthorst's
famous painting

I saw it
again
in the National Gallery
its size—
huge—
always surprises me
its simplicity
too
somber browns
and reds
men looming
from shadows

and in the
center a
candle flares
its light
falling on the
High Priest
who sits
his elbow
resting on
a table
his arm raised
his index finger

A Christian in London & Paris

pointing up
light falls
on the open
Book
before him

it falls
too
on Christ
standing
head
slightly bent
it seems
as if the
High Priest
is saying
don't you know
God's Word
says

and the
Word
the Light
of the world
looks at him
in pity

I saw it
in a room
hanging
on a side wall

A Christian in London & Paris

later
walking into
another room
at right angles
to the first
I saw it
through an arch
at the center
of the far end
forming the focus
of that room

it was
as if
light fell
on me

heedless
of all the
other paintings
in that room
I hurried
to have
another look
crying
silently
Christ
my center
my focal point!
I'll never
hang
you
on a side wall
again!

London—a gourmet's delight

London—
a gourmet's delight
a guzzler's downfall
a slimmer's despair

food fascinating food!
cooks' books glut
bookshops' shelves
every week
new tastes
from somewhere

Harrods' foodhalls
Fortnum and Mason
for the epicure
Tesco
and Sainsbury
for Monday to Friday
for a painless trip
east or west
there are
restaurants galore
east and west
are worlds apart?
they're not
in London

A Christian in London & Paris

my grandmother
I suppose a
typical London girl
grew up in
Victorian Highgate
she packed her bags
left for the
mission field
never lived
in London again
I saw
strange fetishes
she collected
from foreign tribes

London
went everywhere
then
now
everywhere
has come to London
see the turbans
bright African dress
saris and scarves
on the streets

they're not foreign
they're British

hold fast
to the faith
the sea swells

A Christian in London & Paris

the mission field
has come to
London
but is
London
the mission field?

No Haussmann

no Haussmann
laid a logical
level hand
on London

entranced
I sit
in a bus
staring out
and up
up to the tops
of buildings
flowing
like an
intricate
elaborate script
turrets, domes
pinnacles
scrolls
attic windows
pediments
cornices
flat angular tops—
London's
history
is written
in her skyline—
it mesmerizes me

A Christian in London & Paris

others
equally entranced
plod pavements
peering into
plate-glassed fronts
longing
for a world
of things
they'd never
imagined before
cutlery with
yellow handles
and white spots
mugs
with funny farm
animals
books
walking-sticks
tartans and cashmere
galore—
they walk
as if
in a dream

on getting off
the bus
I climb
the steps up
Hungerford Bridge
go halfway
stop and stare
up the Thames to
Big Ben

A Christian in London & Paris

Westminster
Millbank Tower
postmodern MI6
repeat the process
on the other side
staring down
the Thames to
St Paul's
Tower 42
Swiss RE "Gherkin"
Barbican
Tate Modern

two views
of London's
magnificent skyline
so beautiful
and yet so plain
so very very small
beneath
the grandeur
of the arching sky

like lightning
things flash
into perspective
things
have crowded out
the sky!

like
pressure
possessions

A Christian in London & Paris

pleasure
can crowd
God
out of view

Piccadilly Circus

Piccadilly Circus
guide books say
shabby
drugs
promiscuity
but in the
center
Eros

it is
early morning
night revelers
have staggered off
only the odd
person emerges
from the underground
the march
of black-suited
businessmen
strutting
heads high
women
heads bent
clutching computer bags
tourists—
we must see
Eros—
dodging
buses, taxis

A Christian in London & Paris

the preacher
shouting
over and over
Jesus
makes a difference
all these
are not there
early morning

and
I can look at
Eros
moving swiftly
huge wings
outstretched
bow in hand
Eros
Greek god of love?

no!
not at all
he's actually the
Angel
of Christian Charity—

flying over
Piccadilly

The Women of World War II

it was a damp
May morning
the sun shrouded
by dark clouds
about to burst
black umbrellas
everywhere

it suited
the dull grey
monument
stark
in the
center of
Whitehall

smooth as a
gravestone
the line of
faceless women
strung in space
empty uniforms
hung helmets
stench of war
while grief
a violin high-pitched
vibrates
lingeringly
down empty years

A Christian in London & Paris

I stop
remember
the faceless
nameless
women of World War II
they served
they gave
they died
unknown
to those who now
pass them by

and
I remember
the faceless
nameless
Christian women
the centuries of pain
the tired hands
serving
the unknown
deeds done
the silent prayers
becoming
incense
before their
Lord

Berwick Street Market

we chose
the wrong day
for Berwick
Street Market
little on display
peaches past
sell by date
bought a bunch
of rhubarb
though

on the way
through
small streets of
Soho sleaze
fashion
film
gay
I saw another
London—
just as well
for starry-eyed
I forget
too often
London also
has a hell

A Christian in London & Paris

on holiday
in the fifties
my parents
sisters and I
went to see a
London play
at the start—
a rather risqué
part—
my father—
sergeant-major
in the war—
stood up
puffing
grunting
commanded
loudly
come on girls!
out
we traipsed

in the late sixties
living in London
he gave
us tickets
for his
favorite show
I can still see
the fiddler
playing
on the roof

A Christian in London & Paris

what shows
did you see
in London?
asked a friend
on our return

none
I replied
I wasn't sure
what
I would see—

and
I wouldn't
like to be
two-eyed
in hell

London was suffering

London
was suffering
from soccer fever
there was
no vaccine
against that
this year

at first
I wondered why
St George's Cross
was everywhere
proudly flying
on Admiralty Arch
proudly fluttering
from delivery vans
proudly held
in children's hands
skipping
down The Mall
proudly emblazoned
on T-shirts
white with
red cross
reinforced fortissimo
by fans
in open top bus
blaring their hope

A Christian in London & Paris

round Trafalgar Square
and by shop windows
filled with footballs
and men
skillfully aiming
a kick
while Harrods
had a woman
with flaming red hair
draped boldly
over gigantic
gold ball—
England's hope
was palpable
pressure and pulse
ran high

but England's hope
is not winning
the cup
is not the flag
flying everywhere
it's the
cross at the center
which will
make her whole—

Lord
resuscitate
England's
Christian soul!

London's basements

London's basements
below street level
fascinate me

as I walk
past
black spiked
railings
I peer down
steps
into tiny
courtyards
and wonder
about the rooms
beyond

some are
slick offices
well-lit
with large windows
piles of paper
computers
files

others are
drab and dreary
forlorn pots pushed
in corners

A Christian in London & Paris

their plants
long dead
refuse overflowing
rubbish bins

others are
charming
with tubs of flowers
and hanging baskets
rainbow splashes
below
grey streets

in one basement
I know
a pianist lived
with grand piano
antique books
and ancient
oriental carpets

in another
Bayswater
breakfast room
I remember
miniature azaleas
blooming pink
in bright
brass bowls

basements—
basically the same
but

A Christian in London & Paris

some beautiful
some neglected
some simply slums—

depend
on what
the owner's done

Diana

he came
up to us
and said
you from
Sowf Affwica?
you tell 'em
she were murdered
she were

but Diana
still walks
the streets
of London

I saw her everywhere

plaques set
in pavements
inscribed
Diana
Princess of Wales Walk

she smiles
radiantly
from postcard stands

her clothes
on view
in Kensington Palace

A Christian in London & Paris

coming from
the VAT Refund
in Harrods'
basement
I saw
Diana
in a crypt
candle lit
leaning forward
enigmatically
tourists
taking shots

one bleak day
we saw
her memorial
in Hyde Park
no children
were in sight

the fountain—
ring-shaped
turbulent
running swiftly
over smooth
and rocky beds
beside the lake
where she jogged
and now
we walk
her walk—
touched me
poignantly

A Christian in London & Paris

millions of words
have been written
about Diana
truths
half truths
plain lies

yet
when I
think of her
I think
of the joy
she brought
the good
she did

and I wish
I had
prayed
for her
more

Christian art

this time
we didn't
go to
Tate Modern
although
I would have
liked to see
the building
once again—
a disused
power station
turned
spectacular
gallery
I also
would have
liked to lunch
in the
rooftop restaurant
and seen the view—
the Thames and London
stretched out
far below—
but why
I really
go to galleries
is quite simply
to see some
Christian art

A Christian in London & Paris

so we went to
Tate Britain
and the
National Gallery
we saw
the paintings
we love
Christ in the garden
holding a hoe
Mary kneeling
at his feet
and on a
distant hill
three trees
in a row
we had a
photo taken
years ago

this time
we brought home
Jesus
washing
Peter's feet—
it meant
three trips
to the Tate—
but now
hanging in our home
Christ
on one knee
dressed in green
with Peter's
bare foot

A Christian in London & Paris

in his hand
and Peter sitting
perplexed
and slightly
disapproving—
it is a sermon
every day
that's why
Christian art
is art's
greatest form—

the tragedy is
there's so
little of it
today

London's heart

London's heart
was hospitalized
2012
was looming

we found
Nelson encased
in a cast
department stores
bandaged
in billowing plastic
scaffolding
slogans read
open for business
as usual
240 Regent Street
history in the making
even the
Festival Hall
was suffering
was silent
and a
gaping wound
had appeared
next to St Martin's
but the
prognosis was good
a garden
was planned

A Christian in London & Paris

they called
London's cure
renovation
restoration
conservation

rather like
redemption
I thought

When we're back

when we're back
they'll ask
what did you
like best?

well
spiritually

communion
at Holy Trinity
the pathos
of Negro spiritual
St Martin's evensong
the soprano
cascading the nave
while light shone
through the
brilliant blue cross
a duck
waddling in water
amazed
at its coloring—
just a duck—
I praised

then
physically

A Christian in London & Paris

the buildings
the old, the new
medieval St Helen's
a step from
soaring glass Gherkin
the bridges
all different
like jeweled strands
across the river
the London Eye
was the Thames
ever without it?
the parks
their trees
tall and green
as never seen
in our part
of Africa
the grass
soft as baby's hair
woven with
white daisies

what did
I like best?
far easier
to say what
I liked least

as it is
to say about
a fellow
Christian

Regent's Park

London
was drooping
under a
mid June
heat wave
tourists trudged
bottled water
in hand
newspaper stands
proclaimed
drought
the bus to
Regent's Park
was suffocating
only tiny top
windows
could open

but the
roses in
Queen Mary's Garden
thousands
upon thousands
of them
loved it
lifting radiant
faces
to the sun
huge beds

A Christian in London & Paris

             in single colors
             radiated
             from the center
             red, orange
             pink, white
             gold
             the whole
             ringed
             by dancing
             garlands
             strung from
             columns
             hung
             with myriad
             pale roses
             we stood
             stared
             stunned
             at such beauty

             I saw
             other visitors
             stunned too

             the massed beds
             became a
             massed choir
             praising
             lifting
             their fragrance
             to God

Mid May to mid June

mid May
to mid June
the month
of horses
of flags flying
down The Mall
of soldiers
in ceremonial dress
red and gold
and black busbies
of tubas
glinting in the sun
of pageantry
of monarchy

twice
we came upon
such scenes
unexpectedly

we'd planned
to walk
late afternoon
through St James's Park
along the lake
across the bridge
lingering halfway
at the views

A Christian in London & Paris

instead
we watched
Beating the Retreat
that night
I couldn't sleep
I saw
black horses
dancing in formation
heard the bands
the drums
pulsating
the last post's
piercing cry

next day
we planned
a morning walk
past the Palace
to Victoria Station
we like
the hubbub there
we would eat
a baked potato
filled with
cottage cheese
and chives
shop at M & S
ride back

instead we saw
soldiers spaced
along The Mall
like tin soldiers

A Christian in London & Paris

come to life
it was a
dress rehearsal
for
Trooping the Colour

distantly
we heard
approaching music
shouts
of sergeants-major
then we saw
the marching troops
the bandsmen
on black horses
playing joyfully
and in between
the empty carriage
of the Queen

unplanned
we witnessed
unexpected
pageantry

and men shall plan
shall give in marriage
as in Noah's day
heedless
of the greatest glory
the world
will ever see

A Christian in London & Paris

      Christ the King
      coming
      with all the
      hosts of heaven

      unexpectedly

Paris

St-Germain-des-Prés

it's the narrow
winding streets
like streams
at the bottom
of chasms
that I love

with apartments
above
and shops below
the unexpected
everywhere—
a small window
filled with frogs
one
head thrown back
tonks his piano
with much aplomb—
the ormolu clocks
ornate mirrors
and all those
cafés
basking in the sun
pâtisseries
with cakes to rival
Ascot's hats
the food and flowers
in *rue de Buci*
no chicken

A Christian in London & Paris

tastes like one
bought there
with hot potatoes
off the spit
the ancient
books and maps
dusty behind
closed doors
the crowds
cascading
down the streets
all day
and late at night
the quiet
of early morning
when *Madame*
walks her dog
and buys her bread
and eats it
on the way back home

I could quite happily
live there
but I
am here
at Africa's end
where gulls wheel
and waves crash
at my front door

and I am sure
you
put me here

A Christian in London & Paris

there's more to
life than location—

but
thank you
Lord
for such a vacation

St-Germain-des-Prés: an area on the Left Bank named after a church
pâtisseries: cake shops
rue de Buci: Buci Street

Rushing somewhere

Paris

people pressed
like *baguettes*
in a basket
packed boats
parade the *Seine*
stupefied faces
peer from coaches
crowds consume
croissants and salad
squashed on
postcard-sized chairs

the striding young
the old
hobbling on cobbles
the poor
the rich
all rushing somewhere

not to churches
in the squares
except *Notre-Dame*
to see the
rose windows
St-Sulpice
St-Eustache
St-Séverin

A Christian in London & Paris

all silent
neat row
upon row
of empty chairs

a few candles
flicker
faintly in quiet
a few come
to pray
a few to stare
at vaulted naves
precariously high

few see
the crosses
hung
on the walls

and the world
rushes by—
cry
cry

Notre-Dame: Our Lady (cathedral)

Place Dauphine

the crowd
jostling across
Pont-Neuf
past
Henri IV
on his horse
seem unaware
of *place Dauphine*
a secluded square
serene with
chestnut trees
just there
beyond the ancient
red-brick buildings

a couple of *cafés*
serving
tarte tatin
a waitress
hanging flower baskets
in the sun
an old man
nonchalantly
loosening his dog
under the trees
and looking away
a woman
with a walking-stick
on a bench

A Christian in London & Paris

glancing rapidly
up and down
sketching
an artistically
dingy façade
and a young girl
walking swiftly
down one side
of the *place*
head high
her hand
accustomed
and outstretched
tentatively touching
walls
until she disappears
in the crowd
crossing
Pont-Neuf

is she walking
in a world
of darkness
on a
World Heritage Site—
like those
who walk in darkness
when they could
walk in light?

Place Dauphine: Dauphine Square
Pont-Neuf: New Bridge
tarte tatin: Tatin Tart (an upside-down apple tart)

Joan of Arc

I found her
at last
in *musée d'Orsay*
she's not here
she's at the
Louvre
they said

yet
there she sat
apart
from twisted torsos
nudes
fierce faces

Joan
monumental
in size
simplicity
far-seeing eyes

I wondered
who had sat
for her

her simple
pose
soft clothes

A Christian in London & Paris

a young
strong face
a face of faith
of peace
of Christian grace

there wasn't
a picture of
her
in the shop

musée d'Orsay: Orsay art museum
Louvre: Louvre art museum

Roissy-Charles de Gaulle Terminal 2

an architectural
masterpiece
Roissy Terminal 2

we walked
through its
immensely long tunnel
simply lovely
interesting
views over terminal
fields
so peaceful
for an airport
so light
costly

headlines
a week later
Roissy: le scénario du drame
whole section
collapsed
miraculously
only five dead
warning given
falling sand
noise
evacuation

A Christian in London & Paris

    and I remembered
    praying for protection
    changing dates
    we were not there—
    that day

le scénario du drame: the scene, scenario of the tragedy

Place des Vosges

a shot from a helicopter
would be best
it's impossible to get one
that does justice
to the vast *place des Vosges*

the foreground
is cluttered with cars
studios, shops
waiters in white aprons
picnickers in the park
children scrunching
on the gravel
people taking
a quick shortcut
while in the
ancient arcades
a soprano sings arias
a quartet plays Bach
so fitting for this
evocative
French, formal
aristocratic square

unlike most Paris squares
it is a square
nine pink brick mansions
define each side
their slate roofs

A Christian in London & Paris

    encircling it
    like a silver coronet
    the park outlined
    by avenues of linden trees
    trimmed as if
    a giant hand
    had sliced them smooth
    and in the center
    proud and high above
    Louis XIII surveys the scene

    and so
    I never got a shot
    but I shall always remember
    that it reminded me
    of mansions
    of many mansions
    of one with a
    place prepared by you
    in your mercy
    Lord
    for me

Place des Vosges: Vosges Square

Clocks

both beautiful
both spectacular
the two huge clocks
in the old
railway station
which now
majestic
as *musée d'Orsay*
houses art

the first
ornately golden
in the great
vaulted sculpture
gallery

the second
simpler
in the restaurant
on top

it took
much longer
than we thought
to reach the restaurant
we found it full
beneath the clock
but glancing up
I saw a mezzanine

A Christian in London & Paris

cafeteria
coffee machine

it was
quiet there
we chose
baguettes and cheese
and *tarte aux fraises*
and found a table
set as if for us
centered on the clock

and what a view!
its face
sheer glass
showed part of Paris
beyond these
shaded rooms—
vibrant
bright
river
trees
buildings
buses
sun—

like the view
through time
to eternity
now seen in part
but there

baguette: a French stick (bread)
tarte aux fraises: strawberry tart

Jardin des Plantes

it was hot
an old garden
jardin des Plantes
with its
avenues of trees
appealed

they were all there

runners
intent or talking
light of foot
or panting slow
children
chewing chicken
sandwiches
with their teachers
near the swings
or curious
wandering
round the zoo
tourists
maps in hand
heads well-hatted
trudging to the
Grande Galerie de l'Évolution
gardeners
dirty at their

A Christian in London & Paris

daily grind
digging flower beds
snipping off
dead heads
Parisians
simply lazing
in the sun

and she was there
a nun at prayer
still, secluded
book in hand
against the ancient
cedar

for 270 summers
it has stood
in sun and snow
growing slowly
every year
into a
massive monumental
trunk
with branches
that embrace the sky

glancing up
I saw myriad leaves
dark green and delicate
outlined against
the blue
in such a pattern
I have never seen

and after that
I did not dream
of visiting
the evolutionary
museum

Jardin des Plantes: botanical garden
Grande Galerie de l'Évolution: Great Evolutionary Gallery in the Natural History Museum

Les Égouts

dark
dank
a walk
above a sewer
no thank you!
les égouts
pooh!

pallid
sewermen
fetid air
filth is fun?
hold your nose!

but
in the sun
seamy sewers
Pigalle in parts
some TV shows

a booming business
assailing souls

Les Égouts: the sewers

Bus 75

sitting on bus 75
from *parc de la Villette*
to *Pont-Neuf*
looking idly out
in case I missed
something—
something different
from home—
looking at the
young woman
sitting opposite
wondering
is she French?
Algerian? both?
when suddenly
a woman screamed

dumpy
fortyish
furiously spewing
fast French
at a slight
bewildered man
edging away
between the passengers
clutching his hat
repeating *non! non!
non! non!*
as she jabbed

A Christian in London & Paris

her fingers at him
beside herself

the passengers began
to smile surreptitiously
then to laugh
to talk to each other

the bus stopped
the man
the woman
got off
she still shrieking
he vanishing
the passengers
laughing, talking
all the way
to *Pont-Neuf*

it's the Latin in us
said the
young woman to me
we can't help it

change one word
in that sentence
it's the Christian in us
we can't help it—

in other contexts
of course!

parc de la Villette: Villette Park
Pont-Neuf: New Bridge

Early morning walk

Paris
was just waking
the *quai de Conti*
was deserted
even the pleasure boats
were asleep
after a long night

a couple
patting their dog
surrounded
by potted plants
sat on a
moored barge
eating breakfast
while a working barge
large and
hauling heaps of sand
moved swiftly
under the bridges

crossing the *Seine*
on the
wooden footbridge
I stopped to stare
at *Notre-Dame*
and turning
saw the *Tour Eiffel*
the pink dawn sky

A Christian in London & Paris

tinged the water
towering above
quays
façades
island
poplar trees

a woman
was painting the scene
and a couple
hand in hand
wandered across
daytime Paris
seemed far away
this was the time
to stop, to stare

but on the planks
of the bridge
someone had scrawled
in black
cocaine
cannabis
crack
and his name

and on the other side
near the *Louvre*
a tramp
young, mad
shouting, smelling
weaved along
the urine-stained street

A Christian in London & Paris

and I thought
of the views
from the bridge
of the *Parisii*
settling on the island
centuries ago
of the medieval houses
huddled around *Notre-Dame*
of the jets
just starting
to brush white strokes
across the pink
of the future
of change—

the only constant
in this scene
is the sky encompassing all—

like you
unchanging
ever here

quai de Conti: Conti Quay
Seine: the river Seine
Tour Eiffel: Eiffel Tower

Hotel

I read
avidly
lists of hotels
chose one—
delightful description
of itself—
checked with three guides

small
luxurious
wonderful position
ancient building
deluxe room
comfortable

I saw
the ancient—
some blackened beams
tacked on walls—
certainly
not luxurious
certainly small
the four-poster
occupied the room
couldn't unpack

we left
the next day
for another hotel

A Christian in London & Paris

Satan also sells
false information
leave immediately
or inhabit hell

A day in Paris

if *I* had
only a day
in Paris
I would hop
on *les bus*
L'Open Tour
see the sights
jumping frenetically
on an off

if *I* had
only a day
in Paris
I would
sit in the sun
on top of *Printemps*
admire the view
shop in
les grands magasins

if *I* had
only a day
in Paris
I would run to
Montmartre
peep at *Pigalle*
see *Sacré-Cœur*
choose
Moulin Rouge

A Christian in London & Paris

if *I* had
only a day
in Paris
I would
cruise the *Seine*
on a huge *bateau*
under gilt bridges
built for
les rois et les reines

if *I* had
only a day
in Paris
I would
sit on a *terrasse*
on *place des Vosges*
sip *vin rouge*
stare

if *I* had
only a day
in Paris
I would climb
the narrow spiral
into *Sainte-Chapelle*
think of the
crown of thorns
pray

I have
only a day

it's my choice

A Christian in London & Paris

les bus L'Open Tour: city touring buses
les grands magasins: department stores eg *Printemps*
Sacré-Cœur: Sacred Heart (a church)
Moulin Rouge: Red Windmill (cabaret)
bateau: boat
les rois et les reines: kings and queens
terrasse: open-air area of a restaurant
vin rouge: red wine
Sainte-Chapelle: Holy Chapel

Portrait

the *musée de Carnavalet*
housed in two
Renaissance mansions
in the *Marais*
where once
Madame de Sevigné lived
indulgently
luxuriously
writing letters
to her daughter
has much on display—
a grim prison
the *Bastille*
relics of *la Révolution*
some guillotines
lurid scenes of slaughter
a golden toothbrush
in Napoleon's canteen
the street signs
of shops and inns
rescued from
Haussmann's great revamp
and all those portraits
artists were not kind
sitters blind
not to notice
pride
self-satisfaction
cunning

A Christian in London & Paris

cruelty
and now they hang
hardly seen
by tourists
and school children
tramping past

I wonder what
their lives were worth?
I must not say

how would an artist
portray me?

how will
you
on Judgment Day?

Marais: an historic area on the Right Bank
musée de Carnavalet: Carnavalet Museum

Just consider

Paris
city of fashion
city of food
of millionaires in Mercedes
of placards
J'ai faim

just consider food
rues like rainbow ribbons
on market day
figs from France
luscious, black
rose-red raspberries
and lettuce green
and tutu frilly
asparagus
white in bundles
bound in straw
a splash of orange
a dash of cherries
and then ice cream
Berthillon
in every color
pink, pistachio green
cones like castles
caramel crowned, supreme
and then *pâtisseries*
where gaudy *gâteaux*
rival jewelry shops

A Christian in London & Paris

or visit *Bon Marché*
where a queen
could choose her menu
for a palace party—
or restaurants
does eighteenth century appeal?
or *brasseries?*
or *Belle Époque?*
or in a park or gallery?
or *crêpe*
with fried eggs
on the street?

just consider fashion
jumble sale
last year's things
hems have gone mayhem
black and beige
have crept off stage
into center place have leapt
peacock eastern colors

and then
the bags, the belts
the hats, the shoes
the scarves
the jewels—
for an individual look
rush to *Printemps*
Samaritaine
Galeries Lafayette
with pink-gold dome
and all designer labels
or that small *boutique*

with a single satin dress
camellias scattered
on the floor

or
rich and poor
alike

just consider lilies
the lilies of the field

J'ai faim: I am hungry
Berthillon: famous ice cream shop
pâtisseries: cake shops
gâteaux: cakes
Bon Marché, Printemps, Samaritaine, Galeries Lafayette: names of department stores
brasserie: café-restaurant
Belle Époque: beautiful style (early twentieth century style)

Citizens

strange to find
some places
so different
from posters

I found
the *jardins du Trocadéro*
once more
disfigured
last time
scaffolding
this time
skateboarding

place St-Sulpice
covered
crowded
crammed
with white tents
sales, events

I'm glad
I left before the
Seine turned
Midi with palms
sunbathers

A Christian in London & Paris

Paris
is certainly
for its citizens
though tourists
are welcome there

unlike
the glorious
City of God
which says

only citizens here

jardins du Trocadéro: Trocadéro Gardens
place St-Sulpice: St Sulpice Square
Midi: south of France

Jardin du Luxembourg

I found the lovely
jardin du Luxembourg—
Paris's central green space—
unchanged
with Marie de Médicis' palace
now senators'
meeting place
the round pond
for prams
and little Parisians
to sail their yachts
all day
the fountain and lawn
for *Sorbonne* students
to relax from *l'université*
the walks
tennis courts
playgrounds
for fun
the intimate gardens
with statues in shade
to rest or read
Le Monde
the bandstand
the trees
the *café*—

it's the perfect garden
for everyone—

no
Eden was that

Jardin du Luxembourg: Luxembourg Garden
l'université: the university
Le Monde: The World (a daily newspaper)

The Kiss

no not *Rodin's*
a jeans-jacketed
item in
place de la Sorbonne

she
tremulous
giving
as *Rodin's*
Camille

he
eyes roving
alert
pats her
doglike

Hugo
could have hazarded
a hundred
scenes

but I
wept
for her

Rodin: a sculptor. *The Kiss* (a couple entwined in an embrace) is one of his works
place de la Sorbonne: Sorbonne Square
Camille: Rodin's model and mistress
Victor Hugo: an author

Plaques

walking in Paris
I noticed
many enameled plaques
on walls
in most unlikely places
small plaques
each with a name

was she carrying
information
about the foe?
was he creeping
across the bridge
hidden by the dark?
was he helping
a Jew escape?

I will never know

but those who do
hang flowers
near these plaques
which say
so starkly
killed
and give the date

and some
so young

A Christian in London & Paris

to lose
their lives
for liberation

these plaques
more poignant
than all the
pomp and glory
of splendid monuments

and on a
cosmic scale
you came—

to suffer
liberate
reclaim

The new Paris

the new Paris
La Défense
the new towers
where commerce is king
walls of glass
of mirrors
geometric shapes
services
out of sight
underground
bus stations
métro, roads

above
the esplanade
is spacious, calm
with not a
crowded sidewalk
and crowning all
an empty marble cube
vast and proud
its blank face
like an anthill
hides activity
La Grande Arche
modernity
resplendent

A Christian in London & Paris

this time
we did not visit
but saw it
unexpectedly
from a bus
it suddenly was there
huge, shimmering
radiant in the sun
overwhelming
and so near
we passed it quickly
I could only say
look! look!
La Grande Arche!
and it was gone
more beautiful
than when we
spent a day
in glass lift
shooting to the top

I thought
I knew it
but only on the bus
did I truly
see its beauty
so near
and in the sun

then I thought
of the City of God
of new Jerusalem
which will need

no sun
of the unimaginable beauty
of God's glory
which will light it

La Défense: name of the modern business sector of Paris
métro: subway
La Grande Arche: The Great Arch

Doors

there are
no side doors
and the
double doors
high and arched
in the
narrow streets
of old Paris
with their rounded
dented
brass knobs
and peeling paint
in browns and greens
or newly glossed
maroon
present private
forbidding faces

there are
odd glimpses
gone too soon
for peering
passersby
of courtyards
corridors
or staircases
as people
buzz, knock
and slip inside

A Christian in London & Paris

yet
on another level
I see some
poor souls
groping
for side doors
when there are
none

there is but
one Door
which now
flung open
stands
wide and welcoming

Traffic jam

the bus stopped
a traffic jam
the hooting began

I craned my neck
around the
fat woman
to see the cause

a procession
was passing
quietly from the
Cathédrale de Notre-Dame
down *boulevard St-Michel*

the people on the *place*
clicking cameras
the students
chatting
the lone drummer
below the fountain
crowned with the saint
slaying a dragon
all turned and stared

the procession
robed in white
passed—
incongruous

A Christian in London & Paris

but necessary
were the
colored backpacks
bottles of water
the odd umbrella

had they
been slaying
a dragon too?

boulevard St-Michel: St Michel (Michael) Boulevard

Views

we had *café crème*
and *tarte aux poires*—
with rosemary—
on the *terrasse*
on top of *Samaritaine*
sitting beside
flower boxes
filled with herbs
overlooking the *Seine*
splendid with
bridges, turrets
sculptured façades
Notre-Dame
Tour Eiffel
and there
just below
the church of kings

next week
we lunched
on top of *Printemps*
under sunshades
in the sun
the view stretching
from city roofs
and city domes
to *Sacré-Cœur*
white on the *Butte*

A Christian in London & Paris

two spectacular views
of a city
so far from
so different from
so much bigger
than mine

but not nearly
as spectacular
as the view you had

what did you think—
coming from Nazareth—
when high on a
mountain top
the grandeur of Rome
the great cities of the East
the glory of Greece
perhaps Paris
London, New York—
without churches—
were laid before you?

I know what
you said
your stern rebuttal
to the prince
of this world
Away from me, Satan!
for this was a battle
of principalities

A Christian in London & Paris

    of powers in high places
    which you
    as man
    won for us

café crème: espresso with milk
tarte aux poires: pear tart
Butte: a mound on *Montmartre* hill

Parc de Bagatelle

this time
I was determined
to visit
Bagatelle rose garden

early June
roses in full bloom
the day sunny
idyllic

it had looked
easy
but on getting
off the bus
we lost our way

a woman
gave directions
we got
surprisingly near
saw two signs
Bagatelle

chose wrongly
suffice it to say
we walked
we walked
we walked
round the wall

A Christian in London & Paris

but never got in
though I smelt
the scent
of a million roses
just there
over the wall

sunny became
sweltering
my mood
I would rather
not say
let's give up and go!
no, let's try again!

we met two
young women
we're lost! they said
but they'd been
to *Bagatelle*!

I gripped my stick
gritted my teeth
plodded on
their two hundred meters
turned out to be five

but we got there
at last
I saw the *château*
with roses in front
high on a hill
I cannot describe
the colors

A Christian in London & Paris

the scent
the beds
and the garlands
the roses
perfect, open
welcoming us

if I ever go back
now I know the way
I will sit
in that earthly
heaven all day
I will sit
and will praise
I sought
and I found
despite
the wrong turns
wandering around

Parc de Bagatelle: Bagatelle Park
château: castle

References

Page 3: What good will it be for a man if he gains the whole world, yet forfeits his soul? (Matt 16:26 NIV)

Page 9: six days you shall labor (Ex 20:9 NKJV)
the seventh (Ex 20:10 NKJV)

Page 12: still waters (Ps 23:2 KJV)
he restores my soul (Ps 23:3 NIV)
(Poem has: you restore my soul)

Page 23: right in the sight of the Lord (2 Chron 24:2 KJV)

Page 78: walk in the darkness (1 John 1:6 NIV)
walk in the light (1 John 1:7 NIV)
(Poem has: walk in darkness walk in light)

Page 84: many mansions (John 14:2 KJV)
prepare a place (John 14:2 KJV)
(Poem has: with a place prepared)

Page 105: Consider the lilies of the field (Matt 6:28 KJV)
(Poem has: just consider lilies the lilies of the field)

Page 122: Away from me, Satan! (Matt 4:10 NIV)
against principalities, against powers (Eph 6:12 KJV)
(Poem has: of principalities of powers)
prince of this world (John 12:31 KJV)

Page 123: in high places (Eph 6:12 KJV)

To order additional copies of this title call:
1-877-421-READ (7323)
or please visit our Web site at
www.winepressbooks.com

If you enjoyed this quality custom-published book,
drop by our Web site for more books and information.

www.winepressgroup.com
"Your partner in custom publishing."